NLP

for Children

This book belongs to

....

Judy Bartkowiak

1

Paperback ISBN 978-1-907685-43-9

ePub ISBN 978-1-907685-44-6

Mobipocket/Kindle ISBN 978-1-907685-45-3

Published in the UK by MX Publishing

335 Princess Park Manor, Royal Drive, London, N11 3GX

www.mxpublishing.co.uk

Cover design by www.staunch.com

MEET JUDY

I wrote this book just for you because you are very special. There is only one of you and I want you to be happy and have everything you want in life – friends, health and for you to do well at school and with your family.

I have four children – Lucy, Alex, Jess and Paul and they all know about NLP. They think it is great fun and I hope you do too.

My job is to help children who sometimes feel a bit sad or angry. Their parents bring them to see me and we do some of the exercises in this book together.

Ask your Mummy or Daddy to help you as you go through the book. If you want to come and see me, ask them to email me at judy@engagingnlp.com.

I have written this book for children like you aged about 5 – 11yrs. If you are older then there is another book called **NLP for Teens** that you might like. Parents can buy **NLP for Parents** and there is even one for your teachers too called **NLP for Teachers**.

It would be lovely if you could email me and tell me what you think of this book. It is good to get feedback because that is how we learn. I will tell you more about feedback later in the book.

ENGAGING NLP

Did you know that every day around us there are millions of things to see and hear and loads of feelings we could have about them.

BUT

at any point in time we only notice 9 of them.

The funny thing is that each of us notices a different 9 things and that is what makes us unique.

What we pay attention to makes us different.

What we say and how we say it makes us different.

What we do and how we do it makes us different

Every day we make choices about what we notice, what we say and what we do.

Sometimes these choices make us happy and sometimes they make us sad.

I want you to learn about how using NLP can help you make choices that make you happy.

CONTENTS

Welcome to NLP. The letters stands for Neuro Linguistic Programming (what a mouthful!).

Neuro means everything that goes on in our head.

Linguistic is everything that comes out of our mouth, the things we say.

Programming is what we do, our patterns of behaviour.

I am going to tell you how you can get the results you want rather than results you don't want.

Please write or draw in this book and make it your own personal book. Write your name on the front.

WORKSHEET 1: HOW DO I LEARN?

Are you like Vicky, Andy or Kevin? Let's read about them so you can decide.

This is Vicky. She loves to draw and paint. She is very pleased with her picture of the house, isn't she?

She wants to look nice and asks her mummy to brush her hair into plaits with ribbons. These ribbons match her dress don't they?

Vicky says 'Look at this, Mummy! Look what I have painted! Can you see my cat Fluffy in the garden?'

She likes her room to look nice and she is very observant – this means that she notices things she sees around her.

So we say she is VISUAL because she thinks in pictures and notices what she sees.

This is Andy. He likes to make lots of noise and he likes music. He plays the drums. Do you like music? What do you play?

He talks a lot and sometimes he shouts because he wants to be heard. He likes to talk with his friends and make a lot of noise.

He likes his Mummy to read to him and he makes all the noises in the stories. He likes stories with cars in them so that he can go 'brrmmm' really loudly and hoot the horn.

Andy says 'Listen to me! Do you like my drumming? Shall we sing a song?'

He is AUDITORY because he notices what he hears.

This is Kevin. He likes to run around. He doesn't sit still for 5 minutes. He is very active.

Today he is playing with his football. He loves to play football with his friends and go to the park. He likes the climbing frame and the slide best. What do you like to play on in the park?

He wants you to play football with him!

Kevin likes skateboarding too and climbing trees, swimming and anything that involves being active.

He is KINAESTHETIC because he notices what he feels and what he does.

What do you like to do? Write a list here of your favourite things or draw some pictures of you doing them.

Who would you like to play with?

Are you more like Vicky or Andy or Kevin?

Are you

- Visual

- Auditory

- Kinaesthetic

Make a circle round the one that fits you or give it a big tick.

If you are visual you will find it easier to read and learn words and times tables by looking at them and making pictures in your head.

If you are auditory you will learn best by saying the words out loud and listening to how they sound. You will learn your tables best by singing them or listening to a CD or you could chant them out loud.

If you are kinaesthetic you will learn to read, spell and do your times tables by practising them lots of times.

BIG CHUNK/ SMALL CHUNK

We call it 'big chunk' if you like to think about the 'big picture' and do not want to know all the little bits of detail.

For example, if your Mum tells you that you are going shopping; that's all you need to know if you are 'big chunk'. A 'small chunk' child would want to know when and where, which shops you are going to and what you are going to buy.

Let's do this little quiz so you can work out which you are.

CHUNK QUIZ

When your teacher is telling you how to do something at school do you want to know all the detail and maybe ask her questions about it?

> Yes – I ask lots of questions

> No – I just have a go at doing it

Do you want to know the rules of a new game or do you just want to play the game and work it out as you go along?

> Yes – I want to know the rules

> No – I just want to get on with it

When you draw a picture do you fill in all the detail and colour it in neatly or do you just draw rough outlines?

> Yes – I want to fill in the detail

> No – I just draw rough outlines

If someone showed you a picture would you notice all the detail in it or just notice what it was a picture of?

Yes – I would notice the detail

No – I would just notice the main subject

If you mostly answered 'Yes' then you are 'small chunk' and like detail. If you sometimes find you are getting a bit caught up in detail, ask yourself 'and what does this mean?'

If you mostly answered 'No' then you prefer 'big picture' thinking. Sometimes though you need to know how you got there so be prepared to figure it out by asking yourself, 'How did I get there?'

CHOICES

Do you like having choices?

When Mum or Dad ask you what you want to do, do you enjoy thinking about all the options? You could go to the park, go swimming, go to the Jungle Gym ……………if this is fun then you are a 'choices' child. If you prefer to just get on and do something and then do something else and not have to think about which you want to do then you are a 'process' child.

One is not better than the other.

Sometimes you may be 'choices' and other times you might be 'process'. The important thing is to know about it so you understand how you learn.

Here's a little choices quiz for you.

CHOICES QUIZ

Do you like to spend time deciding what to do?

Yes

No

Do you like ticking what you want for Christmas in catalogues?

Yes

No

Do you flick through the TV channels to look at all the choices before deciding what to watch?

Yes

No

Do you have lots of friends so you have lots of choice of who to play with?

Yes

No

If you mostly answered 'Yes' then you are 'choices' and if you answered 'No' you are process.

If you like choices you will like to choose for yourself when to do your homework or which topic to write an essay on. If you are process you just want to get on and do it.

In a situation where you are not given a choice, you can give yourself one. You can choose to use this pen or that pen, tidy your room starting at this end or that end, for example. If you don't want choices, just pick the first option you are given to avoid having to choose between lots of options.

TOWARDS/AWAY FROM

Do you think about what you DO want or what you DON'T want?

Do you think about what you want MORE of or what you want LESS of?

19

If you think about what you want and what you want more of, you are a 'towards' child and if you think about what you don't want or what you want less of, you are an 'away from' child.

For example, a 'towards' child will think of what they want for supper and an 'away from' child will hope they don't get something they don't like.

It doesn't matter which you are. Again it helps to know how you learn best. If you are 'towards' you will want to get good marks at school and if you are 'away from' you want to avoid getting bad marks.

Here is another little quiz for you.

TOWARDS/AWAY FROM QUIZ

Do you think about what you want more of or what you want less of?

      A - More of

      B - Less of

In the playground do you look out for children you want to play with or avoid who you don't want to play with?

      A - Look for friends

      B - Avoid who you don't like

Do you behave well to please your Mum or Teacher or because you don't want to get into trouble?

      A - Want to please

      B - Don't want to get in trouble

Do you keep your room tidy because you want to be able to find things or because you'll get told off if it's in a mess?

      A - Want to be able to find things

      B - Don't want it in a mess

If you mostly answered 'A' then you are 'towards' and 'B' you are 'away from'.

Being aware of which you are can help you understand why you feel how you feel and how other people are different.

Both are OK.

If you are 'away from', ask yourself sometimes 'What do I want?' or 'What do I want more of?' because you are more likely to get what you do want than not get what you don't want.

<u>WORKSHEET 2: MAKING FRIENDS</u>

It feels good to have friends doesn't it?

Who are your friends? Draw some pictures of your friends and write their names next to their pictures on the next page.

What do you like about your friends?

I like…………………………………

because she / he is

…………………………………………………

…………………………………………………

I like……………………………….

because she / he is

…………………………………………………

…………………………………………………

I like …………………………………

because she / he is

…………………………………………………

…………………………………………………

Here is a game you can play with a friend, it is called 'mirroring'.

- Sit opposite each other.

- First you do something such as pretend to brush your hair. You can do any action you like. You can make faces or take up a pose.

- Ask your friend to copy what you do in exactly the same way.

- Then they do something and you copy them.

- Do it 5 times each.

Do you end up laughing?

I expect so.

The reason is that doing the same thing as each other makes you feel closer and better friends.

You can do this with children you want to be friends with.

Here is a more advanced version.

- Sit opposite each other.

- Say something to your friend.

- Then ask them to repeat it back to you.

- Now ask them to say something and you repeat it back to them.

- Do it 10 times each.

Do you notice that your friend uses different words from you?

If you are a different VAK (Worksheet 1) from your friend you may use different expressions and different words.

If you have noticed this, do the exercise again and this time when it's your turn use <u>their</u> choice of words and expressions.

Do you notice a difference?

Make a note here.

WORKSHEET 3: HOW TO FEEL HAPPY AGAIN

Do you sometimes feel a bit sad?

When do you feel sad?

Maybe at school sometimes you feel you can't do what the teacher asks?

Perhaps sometimes at home Mummy or Daddy get cross with you?

Wouldn't it be great to have a way to feel magically happy?

I have an exercise for this and it is called 'Anchoring'.

Do you know what an anchor is?

It is a heavy piece of metal shaped like the one above and big ships drop one down into the sea when they want to stop. It falls to the sea bed and digs into the sea bottom with its sharp points so the ship won't sail away.

We can have our own anchor so we can use it when we feel sad and want to feel happy again. You need an anchor.

Draw yours here.

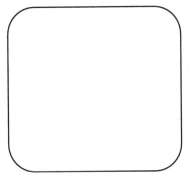

Now you have your anchor we need to give it some magic to make it work.

If you are like Vicky you can picture your anchor and hold that picture in your mind, can't you?

If you are like Andy you may want to say the word 'anchor' when you need to use it.

If you are more like Kevin you may want to squeeze your ear lobe to remind you of your anchor.

Here's what you do next.

Close your eyes and think about a time when you were really happy.

What can you think of?

Was it a good party or playing with your special friend?

Something you did on holiday perhaps?

When you have the picture of that special time in your head, you need to drop your anchor into the sea.

So if you are Vicky, think of the picture of your anchor.

If you are an Andy, say the word 'anchor' and if you are Kevin, squeeze your ear lobe.

Do this a few times and soon you will be able to use your anchor whenever you feel sad.

Whatever you use as your anchor, make sure you do the same thing every time to remember your happy time.

If you have an even happier time you could anchor that and use that one as well.

The secret is to use the anchor to remind yourself of being happy so wherever you are and whatever is happening you can cheer yourself up by dropping your anchor.

Write down here when you could use your anchor.

WORKSHEET 4: CONFIDENCE

Do you know what confidence is?

It is when you feel good about yourself, when you feel OK.

Chris the crocodile is dancing to show us that he feels OK today but he doesn't always feel OK.

Sometimes he feels he is useless at everything and no-one loves him and he has no friends.

Poor Chris!

Do you sometimes feel like that? I do.

What you need to do is have a list that you can stick on your wall that reminds you of all the things you can do.

Let's start that list right now. I'll help you. Can you do any of these things? Put a big tick right next to it if you can.

Touch my nose with my tongue

Do a handstand

Say my name backwards

Tell a joke

Not talk for a whole minute

Draw a picture of myself

Get myself dressed for school

Now you carry on……..

What a lot of things you can do!

Will Mummy let you stick it on your wall so that you can look at it when you feel not OK?

Do you know that every day you are learning to do new things and you are adding to that list?

Things you couldn't do yesterday, you can do today but you must believe you can do them.

Do you ever say 'I can't do that'?

Make a note here of when you say that?

Yes, we all do at some time or other.

When Chris says that, do you know what I say to him?

I say

"But what if you could?"

Then he has a go at it and do you know what?

He can do it after all.

He just thought he couldn't do it because it was new to him and he didn't feel confident.

Next time you think you can't do something, look at your list and think of all the things you can do.

If you can do all those things you can certainly have a go at this new thing.

Do you know why?

Because once you have done it you can add it on to the list and soon your list will be so long it will reach the floor and then travel along the floor and down the stairs and out of the front door.

Your friends will say, what's that?

And your Mum and Dad will say 'Oh that's our child's list of all the things they can do now".

They will say "WOW that's amazing!"

WORKSHEET 5: COPING WITH CHANGE AND GRIEF

Do you ever feel that you want everything to stay the same?

Things change around us all the time and we cannot stop them because we are only children and other people make the decisions, not us.

Perhaps you have had changes in your life that you have been cross about.

When we feel cross we can sometimes be a bit naughty and we don't want to be.

It's because we are upset.

This is Fergus Frog.

He is very grumpy because he has to move house and leave all his friends.

He doesn't want to go.

He doesn't like change.

He says he won't go but he knows that he will have to.

Deep down we know we have to do what we are told even if we don't want to and we feel cross and upset.

So how can we feel better about changes and things we don't like?

41

What we do is jump on the Time Line.

I'll let Steve the Stopwatch tell you all about it.

Hello I'm Steve.

I'm a stopwatch and I live on a Time Line.

A Time Line is an imaginary line that you draw on the floor (not with a felt pen please kids!) and it stands for time.

At one end is when you were very tiny and at the other end is when you are grown up.

Here's what you do.

- Go and stand on the line that represents now, today.

- Tell Steve about what is going on in your life today.

  - What makes you happy and what makes you sad.

  - Who you like and who you don't like.

  - How you feel and what you want to change.
- Now move along the imaginary line to a place on it when you think you will feel a bit happier.

- Tell Steve what's going on now.

    o What has changed?

    o How do you feel now?

- Now go back to where you were. Don't you feel happier knowing things will get better?

You see Steve knows things will get better in time even though they may be horrible now.

You can use your Time Line whenever you want to time travel.

You can go back in time and remember when you were younger or you can go forward in time to imagine how things will be in the future.

Remember to return to today before you get off the line otherwise Steve will have to chase you back and set off his very loud alarm.

WORKSHEET 6 : GOALS

A goal is something you want, not a thing like a new video game or a toy but something like

- Making friends

- Doing well at school

- Swimming a length

- Getting into a school sports team

- Being kind to your baby sister

What is your goal?

Think about what you would like to have as a goal

- At home

- At school

- In your hobby e.g. sport, music, art

Your goal needs to be -

1) POSITIVE

Write your goal down as what you want not what you don't want or want less of. Remember this is a 'towards' goal. It might be a reading level you want to get on or a maths level. Which times table do you want to know well? How many of your spellings do you want to get right next week?

2) How will you know when you have got your goal?

What sign or evidence do you need to show you have achieved your goal?

Is it a mark, a level or a score? Is it some 'A's in your end of term report? Is it getting a part in the school play or a place in the sports team? How will you know you have got your goal? You need to know you have reached it so you can give yourself a pat on the back.

3) What and who do you need to help you?

Ask your parents or your teachers and your friends to help you. Sometimes we need to ask for help and that is a nice feeling. We like to help our friends don't we?

What are you good at that will help you achieve your goal? You can anchor it using the worksheet we have just done.

4) What will be good about getting your goal?

Think about what will be good about achieving your goal and what else you will be able to do once you have achieved it. What might your next goal be?

Use this space to write down your goal

My goal is to ……………………..

WORKSHEET 7: CONTROLLING YOUR MOOD

Another word for mood is 'state' and before we start thinking about how to control it, we need to know what your happy, sad and angry state is. Then we can recognise when we have a problem.

When do you feel happy?

....

....

How are you when you are happy? What do you do? What do you say? What could someone else see?

Draw a picture below.

This is me when I am happy.

And now, when are you angry? What do you say, what could someone else see and what do you feel inside? What do you do?

Draw a picture of you when you are angry or in a bad mood.

And now when are you sad? What do you say,

what do you do and what would someone else see?

Draw a picture of you when you are sad.

Now you know what to look out for when you are in different moods but how do we get rid of the bad mood or the bad state?

Here's how.... let's SWISH the bad stuff away.

This is a really good way to do this.

SWISH IT AWAY!

1) Think about what happens just before you get into a bad mood. This is called 'the trigger'. It's like a switch, we turn it on in our head and 'bang' our mood changes.

   What we need to do is change our reaction to the trigger.

   Is the trigger for you something you see (if you are visual) something someone says (if you are auditory) or something you feel (if you are kinaesthetic)?

Write down what happens just <u>before</u> you feel bad or angry or sad.

The trigger for me is.............................

Then what happens? Write it down here.

2) Make a picture in your head of what happens when you feel really bad and imagine it like a picture on the screen as if it's a movie at the cinema.

3) Now think of what you would like to happen instead next time that trigger goes off in your head. Write it down in the box below.

4) Make a picture in your head of this now. Then place that picture in the bottom left hand corner of the screen with your bad image in it. Like this.

5) Now say out loud 'SWISH' and make the good image in the corner switch with the bad image in the middle like this.

You will need to practice it a few times and when you have it perfect you can use it every time you see, hear or feel that trigger in your head.

You can use this SWISH whenever you want to replace a bad image or idea with a good one.

WORKSHEET 8: COPING WITH CRITICISM

Sometimes you will be told off or criticised and it isn't very nice is it? You have two choices as to how to respond. Before you respond at all – STOP AND THINK

1) Was I in the wrong? If one of my friends saw what I did or heard what I said, would they think I was in the wrong as well?

2) If you think that you were in the wrong and that your friend would also think so then you need to

    a. Apologise

    b. Remember not to do it again.

3) If you don't think you were in the wrong and you don't think your friend would think so either, then you need to explain what happened and why you think you were not in the wrong.

We learn from criticism even if we were not in the wrong because next time we will make sure that we don't repeat the same thing just in case someone thinks we have done something wrong.

Learning from our mistakes is called 'reframing' because what we are doing is taking a bad experience like being told off and using it to learn how to do something different next time.

Here are some other examples of reframing. It is about looking at the positive side of a situation.

Which glass looks half full?

....

Which glass looks half empty?

....

They both have the same amount of juice don't they? It's just a matter of how they look to us.

If you focus on the one that is half full we would say you are an optimist and see the positive side of things.

If you notice more the one that is half empty we would say you were a pessimist and see the negative side of things.

Have a look at some of these situations down the left hand side and think how you could reframe them. Then look at the right hand side of the page to see my reframe suggestion.

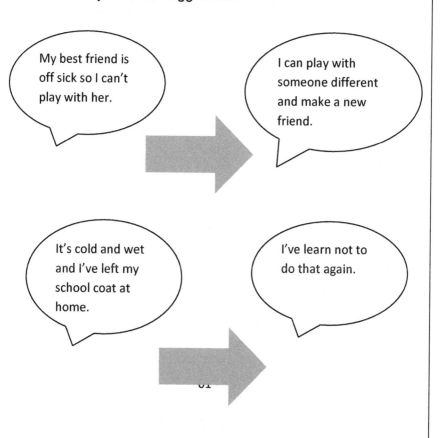

My best friend is off sick so I can't play with her.

I can play with someone different and make a new friend.

It's cold and wet and I've left my school coat at home.

I've learn not to do that again.

You can make a game of it! Next time you feel cross about something or sad, think of how creative you can be and come up with some really good positive thing about it instead.

Imagine how you could reframe the things you don't like doing? Make a list here.

Things I don't like   Reframe it as

TOXIC WORDS

Here are some toxic words that need to be reframed.

TRY

When Mum or Dad or your teacher asks you to try and do something, how hard do you try?

Not very?

That's because when they ask you to try they don't think you will do it. If they did, they would just ask you to do it wouldn't they?

Sometimes we talk to ourselves don't we? Do you say to yourself "I'll try to do it"? That means you won't do it at all. Instead, next time just tell yourself to

DO IT!

CAN'T

Do you sometimes say 'I can't do this or that'? Of course you do! We all say that sometimes.

The trouble is that when we say that we don't even give it a go. If we did, we might surprise ourselves because maybe we can do it after all.

If you don't even give it a go then you can't add it to that list we made earlier of all the things you can do.

It also means that if you 'can't do' that, maybe it could have been fun and now you won't know whether it is or not. You have cut down your choices.

So next time when you tell yourself you 'can't' do something like 'I can't do maths' or 'I can't spell' instead tell yourself

BUT WHAT IF I COULD???

DON'T

If I say to you

"Don't think about pink elephants"

What are you thinking about now?

You have to think of a pink elephant don't you
because otherwise you can't make sense of what I
said. So now you have to not think about them.
How do you 'not think' about something?

Focus on what you do want rather than what you
don't want. Instead of saying to Mum 'Don't put any
tomatoes in my lunch box' tell her what you do want
in it.

It's the same with younger brothers and sisters. If you tell them 'Don't touch my things' straight away they will do it because you have given them that thought. Instead say 'Please play with your own toys'.

AND FINALLY

If there is anything you are unsure about or would like to work on, please get in touch with me judy@engagingnlp.com or via my website www.engagingnlp.com and I would be happy to explain further or arrange an NLP coaching session.

References

NLP at work, Sue Knight, Nicholas Brealey Publishing

Happy Kids Happy You, Sue Beever, Crown House Publications

Brilliant Parent, Emma Sargent, Prentice Hall

The complete secrets of happy children, Steve & Sharon Thorsons, Biddulph

How to talk so kids will listen and listen so kids will talk Adele Faber & Elaine Mazlish, Simon & Schuster Audio

Teach yourself NLP, Steve Bavister & Amanda Vickers, Hodder

Bringing up happy children, Glenda Weil & Doro Marden, Hodder

The Satir Model, Virginia Satir, Science and Behavior Books

Think Good Feel Good, Paul Stallard, Wiley

Seeing Spells Achieving

The UK's leading NLP book for learning difficulties including dyslexia

Stop Bedwetting in 7 Days

A simple step-by-step guide to help children conquer bedwetting problems in just a few days

Recover Your Energy

NLP for Chronic Fatigue, ME and tiredness

Play Magic Golf

How to use self-hypnosis, meditation, Zen, universal laws, quantum energy, and the latest psychological and NLP techniques to be a better golfer

Psychobabble

A straight forward, plain English guide to the benefits of NLP

You Too Can Do Health

Improve Your Health and Wellbeing, Through the Inspiration of One Person's Journey of Self-development and Self-awareness Using NLP, energy and the Secret Law of Attraction

Process and Prosper

Inspiring and motivational book from necrotising faciitis survivor Wendy Harrington. Amazing book for anyone facing critical trauma.

Bangers and Mash

Battling throat cancer with the help of an NLP coach. Keith's story has led to changes in procedure in many cancer hospitals and is an inspiration to cancer patients everywhere.

Performance Strategies for Musicians

Tackle stage fright and performance anxiety using NLP.

9 781907 685439